Big
Science Ideas

Animals without backbones

Bobbie Kalman

 Crabtree Publishing Company

www.crabtreebooks.com

Big Science Ideas

Created by Bobbie Kalman

Dedicated by Crystal Sikkens
To my good friends, Dianne and Stuart Vanderknyff,
congratulations on your new bundle of joy, Darren Stuart!

Author and Editor-in-Chief
Bobbie Kalman

Research
Robin Johnson

Editor
Kathy Middleton

Photo research
Bobbie Kalman
Crystal Sikkens

Design
Bobbie Kalman
Katherine Kantor
Samantha Crabtree (cover)

Production coordinator
Katherine Kantor

Prepress technician
Margaret Amy Salter

Illustrations
Barbara Bedell: pages 13, 15, 23
Antoinette "Cookie" Bortolon: page 4 (boy)
Katherine Kantor: page 4 (bird and frog skeleton)
Bonna Rouse: pages 14, 17, 29
Margaret Amy Salter: pages 4 (turtle skeleton), 5, 24, 25

Photographs
© Dreamstime.com: pages 7 (top), 9 (top), 10 (left), 11 (top),
   12, 17 (right), 22 (top), 27 (top), 28, 31 (top left)
© iStockphoto.com: pages 5 (sea urchin), 18 (bottom)
© Doug Perrine / SeaPics.com: page 31 (bottom)
© Shutterstock.com: front and back cover, title page, pages 4,
   5 (except sea urchin), 6, 7 (bottom), 8, 9 (bottom), 10 (right),
   11 (bottom), 13, 14, 15, 16, 17 (left), 18 (top), 19, 20, 21,
   22 (bottom), 23, 24, 25, 26, 27 (bottom), 29, 30, 31 (top right)

Library and Archives Canada Cataloguing in Publication

Kalman, Bobbie, 1947-
    Animals without backbones / Bobbie Kalman.

(Big science ideas)
Includes index.
ISBN 978-0-7787-3279-2 (bound).--ISBN 978-0-7787-3299-0 (pbk.)

    1. Invertebrates--Juvenile literature. I. Title. II. Series.

QL362.4.K34 2008   j592   C2008-905553-5

Library of Congress Cataloging-in-Publication Data

Kalman, Bobbie.
    Animals without backbones / Bobbie Kalman.
        p. cm. -- (Big science ideas)
    Includes index.
    ISBN-13: 978-0-7787-3299-0 (pbk. : alk. paper)
    ISBN-10: 0-7787-3299-1 (pbk. : alk. paper)
    ISBN-13: 978-0-7787-3279-2 (reinforced library binding : alk. paper)
    ISBN-10: 0-7787-3279-7 (reinforced library binding : alk. paper)
    1. Invertebrates--Juvenile literature. I. Title.
QL362.4.K35 2009
592--dc22
                                          2008036593

Crabtree Publishing Company

www.crabtreebooks.com   1-800-387-7650

Published in Canada
Crabtree Publishing
616 Welland Ave.
St. Catharines, Ontario
L2M 5V6

Published in the United States
Crabtree Publishing
PMB16A
350 Fifth Ave., Suite 3308
New York, NY 10118

Published in the United Kingdom
Crabtree Publishing
White Cross Mills
High Town, Lancaster
LA1 4XS

Published in Australia
Crabtree Publishing
386 Mt. Alexander Rd.
Ascot Vale (Melbourne)
VIC 3032

Contents

Backbones or no bones?

There are many kinds of animals on Earth. Some are **vertebrates**. Vertebrates are animals that have backbones inside their bodies. A backbone is a row of bones in the middle of an animal's back. Vertebrates have many other bones inside their bodies, too. All the bones make up a **skeleton**. A skeleton supports the body. **Muscle**, fat, and skin cover the skeleton.

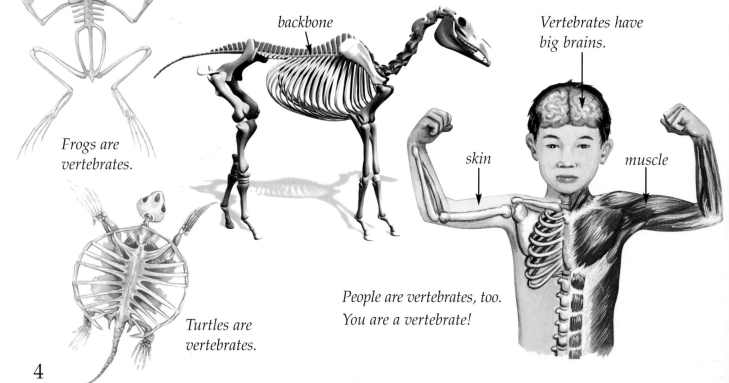

Birds are vertebrates.

Frogs are vertebrates.

Turtles are vertebrates.

Horses are vertebrates.

backbone

People are vertebrates, too. You are a vertebrate!

Vertebrates have big brains.

skin

muscle

Animals without backbones

Most of the animals on Earth do not have backbones. Animals without backbones are called **invertebrates**. There are millions of kinds of invertebrates. All the animals shown on this page are invertebrates.

octopus

spider

sea star

snail

worms

sea urchin

butterfly

crab

Hard and soft coverings

Ladybugs have hard exoskeletons on the outside of their bodies.

This girl is holding a conch shell. Do you think she can hear ocean waves inside it?

Snails have thick, hard shells.

Vertebrates have skeletons made of hard bones. The bones are inside their bodies. Invertebrates do not have hard bones inside their bodies. Their bodies are supported in different ways. Some invertebrates have hard skeletons, called **exoskeletons,** covering their bodies.

Living in shells

Some invertebrates with soft bodies have thick, hard shells. Snails and many sea animals have hard shells that protect their bodies. Most of these animals live inside their shells. Snails come out of their shells to move around and to find food.

No bones

Sea cucumbers live in oceans. They do not have shells. Sea cucumbers have **endoskeletons**. An endoskeleton is hard material under the sea cucumber's skin that gives it support and shape. Some sea cucumbers are shaped like vegetable cucumbers.

*This sea cucumber is called a sea apple. It has **tentacles** at one end of its body. It uses its tentacles to trap food.*

tentacles

Sponges live in oceans

Many invertebrates live in water. Water supports their bodies. Water also carries food. Sponges are invertebrates that live in oceans, but they cannot swim. They stay in one spot. To find food, sponges suck in water through holes in their bodies. They then eat the food that is in the water.

These sponges are tube sponges. They look like plants, but they are invertebrate animals.

Simple bodies

Sponges are invertebrates with simple bodies. They do not have heads, arms, or legs. Sponges have no brains, hearts, or other **organs**, either. Sponges have different shapes. Which sponge looks like a barrel? Which one looks like a vase?

Five parts

Sea stars are star-shaped animals that live in oceans. A sea star has five or more **identical** body parts. Identical means exactly alike. Each part is joined at the center of the body. Sand dollars and sea urchins also have parts that are joined at the middle of their bodies. They belong to the same family as sea stars.

Sea stars have five identical arms.

Sand dollars also have five identical parts.

Spines and shells

Sea urchins and their relatives have **spines** on their skin. Spines are sharp, pointed body parts. They help protect the animals from **predators**. Under their skin, the animals have round, hard shells. The shells have five parts. You can see these parts below.

Some sea urchins have long, sharp spines. The spines cover and protect their bodies.

*This picture shows a sea star with five arms. It also shows the five parts on the round shells of some sea urchins. They all have **fivefold symmetry**, or five identical parts.*

bell

tentacles

*The body of a sea jelly has a **bell** at the top. The bell makes jelly. The mouth and stomach of the sea jelly are inside the bell. The tentacles hang down from the bell. The tentacles are covered with stinging parts.*

Sea stingers

Sea jellies and sea anemones are invertebrates that sting. These animals have soft bodies. Their bodies are made up mainly of a mouth, stomach, and many **tentacles**. The animals use their tentacles to sting and catch **prey** in oceans. Prey are animals that are hunted by other animals called predators.

This sea stinger is a sea anemone. It looks like a flower.

Coral reefs

Corals are made up of tiny animals called **polyps**. Some coral polyps have soft bodies. Other corals make hard skeletons around their bodies. The skeletons protect the polyps from predators. When the polyps die, their skeletons stay in the ocean. New polyps grow on top of the skeletons. After many years, the skeletons pile up and form **coral reefs**.

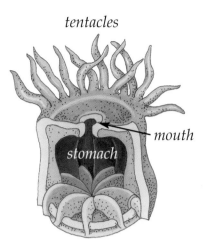

tentacles

mouth

stomach

This coral polyp has a soft, simple body. It has very few parts and no bones.

coral polyps up close

*Coral reefs are the **habitats**, or homes, of many invertebrates and other animals.*

Wiggly worms

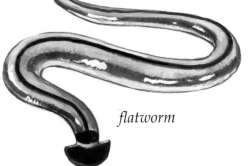

flatworm

Flatworms have thin, flat bodies
that are covered in **mucus**.
Mucus is a sticky, slimy liquid.

roundworm

Roundworms have long, thin bodies.
Most are so small that you need a
microscope to see them.

Worms wiggle from place to place.
They have soft bodies with no arms
or legs. Some worms are made up of
many ring-shaped **segments**, or parts.
Worms use their muscles to stretch or
shrink their segments. They can twist,
turn, slide, and wiggle by making
their segments longer or shorter. The
worms below are using their muscles
and segments to twist and turn.

*You can see the many segments
on the bodies of these earthworms.*

14

Earthworms

Earthworms live in the ground. They have long, thin bodies with many segments. They have no bones inside their soft bodies. Instead of bones, earthworms have skeletons filled with a liquid. Soft skeletons and many segments allow worms to glide easily through soil.

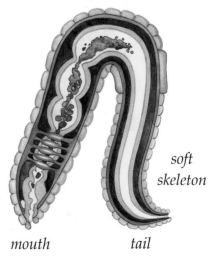

inside an earthworm

soft skeleton

mouth   *tail*

15

Worms in water

Some worms live in the ground, but many types of worms live in water. **Marine** worms live in oceans. Ocean water contains a lot of salt. There are also worms that live in **fresh water**. Ponds, lakes, and streams have fresh water. Fresh water does not have very much salt in it.

There are two kinds of marine worms in this picture. Can you name them? If not, you can find their names on page 17.

Sea mice are not really mice! They are marine worms. Where do these worms live?

fireworm

Bristle worms have many tiny **bristles**, or stiff hairs, on their bodies. This type of bristle worm is called a fireworm.

Leeches are worms that live mainly in fresh water. Some leeches suck blood from animals and people.

Christmas-tree worms live in oceans. They look like colorful trees, but they are invertebrates! Which number was this worm on page 16?

cilia

These are feather-duster worms. They have feathery **cilia** on their bodies. They use the cilia to trap food that floats in the ocean. Did you find the feather-duster worms on page 16?

Slugs and snails

tentacles

foot

Snails and slugs belong to a group of animals called **mollusks**. Mollusks are invertebrates with soft bodies. Most mollusks have hard shells that cover and protect their bodies, but some mollusks do not have shells. Slugs are mollusks without shells.

Most slugs do not have shells. Their wormlike bodies are covered by a thick layer of mucus. The mucus protects the slug from cuts. It also makes the ground under the slug slippery, so the slug can glide over it. This slug is called a banana slug. Why do you think it was given this name?

Slow snails

Snails are slugs with shells. They pull their bodies into their shells to hide from predators. Snails creep slowly through gardens, fields, and forests on one large **foot**. The foot is a soft, strong muscle. It carries a snail from place to place.

*The shell of a snail has a **spiral** shape.*

foot

19

Colorful sea slugs

Nudibranchs are sea slugs, but not all sea slugs are nudibranchs. "Nudibranch" is pronounced "nudi-brank."

What are nudibranchs?

Nudibranchs are mollusks that have no shells. They are the most colorful creatures on Earth! Their colors often blend in with the corals around them. Nudibranchs breathe through the frilly **plumes** on their backs. A nudibranch moves on a foot, the way a land slug moves.

Nudibranchs are colorful invertebrates. They are beautiful ocean animals!

Octopuses and squids

Octopuses and squids are the biggest, smartest invertebrates. They have large brains and very good **senses**. They touch, smell, and taste with **suckers**. Suckers are suction cups on their arms. Octopuses have six arms and two legs. Squids have two long tentacles as well as eight arms.

Octopuses and squids live in oceans. Most live in deep, cold waters.

suckers

22

Defending themselves

Octopuses and squids are mollusks without shells. Some octopuses and squids have shells inside their bodies, but most protect their bodies in other ways. Octopuses and squids change their skin color to blend in with their surroundings. Blending in helps squids and octopuses hide from predators.

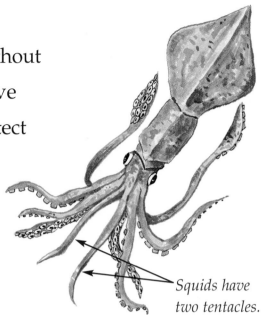

Squids have two tentacles.

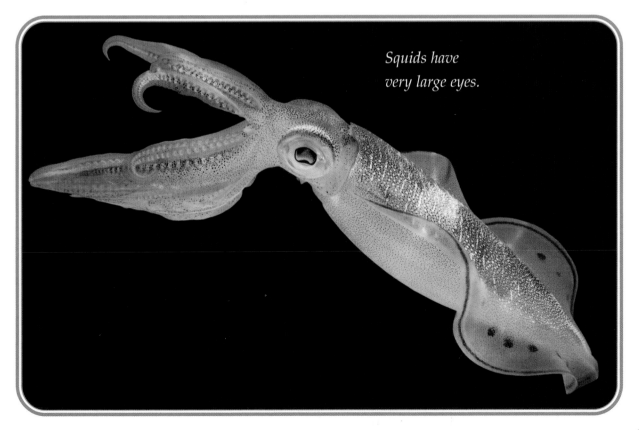

Squids have very large eyes.

23

Crusty crustaceans

lobster

Lobsters, crayfish, and crabs belong to a group of animals called **arthropods**. Arthropods are invertebrates that have exoskeletons on the outside of their bodies. Exoskeletons are made of a tough material called **chitin**. They protect the soft body parts of arthropods.

crayfish

Lobsters, crayfish, and crabs are **crustaceans**. *Crustaceans are arthropods that live mainly in water. Lobsters and crabs live in oceans, but crayfish live in fresh water. Crayfish look like small lobsters.*

Legs that bend

Arthropods have **joints** inside their bodies. Joints are places where two body parts come together. Your elbows and knees are joints. Joints allow arthropods to bend their legs and claws. Crabs and lobsters have ten legs that bend. Their two front legs are claws.

legs

joint

claw

Most crabs have wide, flat bodies and short legs. They use their legs to crawl, swim, and catch food.

Insect invertebrates

grasshopper

Insects are also arthropods. They have hard exoskeletons that cover their small bodies. Insects have six legs that bend. Some insects have short legs. Grasshoppers have long back legs. Long legs help these insects take huge leaps.

Beetles are insects. Many beetles have brightly colored exoskeletons.

Wings to fly

Many insects have wings. Some insects have one pair of wings. Other insects have two pairs of wings. Insects with wings can fly. Insects are the only invertebrates that can fly.

Dragonflies have two pairs of wings.

Insects fly to find food and to escape from predators.
*This butterfly is taking a drink of **nectar**. Nectar is a sweet liquid found in flowers.*

27

Spiders are not insects

Spiders are arthropods, but they are not insects. They do not have wings and cannot fly. Spiders have eight legs that bend. They use their legs to crawl from place to place. This spider is crawling on a flower. It is looking for insects to eat.

Strong silk

Spiders make **silk** inside their bodies. Silk is a very strong thread. Spiders use silk to build homes and to escape from predators. Many spiders also use silk to make sticky webs. The webs trap insects and other small prey.

Some baby spiders shoot long silk threads into the air. The wind catches the silk and carries the spiders away!

This spider has caught an insect in its sticky web.

Did you know?

Invertebrates have many kinds of bodies. They are amazing animals! You have learned much about invertebrates in this book, but there is much more to find out! How many of these facts did you know about invertebrates?

Did you know?
Arthropods outgrow their exoskeletons. They **shed** their old exoskeletons and grow new, bigger coverings.

Did you know?
Some sea jellies make their own light. They light up their bodies to **attract** prey in dark ocean waters.

sea star

Did you know?
Sea stars can grow new arms to replace ones that were hurt or eaten by predators.

spider

Did you know?
Spiders do not chew their food. They turn their prey to liquid and drink their dinner!

giant clam

Did you know?
Some clams are bigger than people! Giant clams are huge mollusks with two big shells.

Glossary

Note: Some boldfaced words are defined where they appear in the book.

attract To make someone or something come closer

cilia Tiny hairlike body parts used to trap food or to move from place to place

coral reef An area in shallow ocean water that is made up of live and dead corals

endoskeleton A hard material under the skin of some animals that supports them and gives them shape

exoskeleton A hard covering on the outside of an animal's body

marine Describing an animal that lives in the ocean

muscle Part of the body that helps an animal move and which gives it strength

organ A body part that does an important job

plume A part of an animal's body that looks like a feather

predator An animal that hunts and eats other animals

sense An ability, such as sight, which helps an animal learn about its world

shed To lose an outer layer or exoskeleton

spiral A circle shape that starts at a center and gets bigger as it curls around and around itself

tentacle A body part near the mouth of an invertebrate that is used for feeling, grasping, or moving

Index

Printed in the U.S.A. - CG